READER, I MARRIED HIM

& OTHER QUEER GOINGS-ON

ACKNOWLEDGEMENTS

Earlier versions of some these poems have appeared in *Scarf: Global Arts & Literature magazine*; *The Poetry Review*; *SABLE Litmag* and "No Condition Is Permanent" (Platform/African Writers Abroad, 2010); "a sense of denial" was originally commissioned as part of "C-Words: Carbon, Climate, Capital, Culture" by Platform/African Writers Abroad (2009); "on arrival at the royal college of music" and "the yellow & black triangles" were originally commissioned as part of "Looking for Samuel" by The Books Project/Victoria & Albert Museum (2012).

I'm thankful for the continued support of my egun, and the Orisha Obatala and Oshun. My thanks as always to my chosen family & lifelong friends: Danny, Jennifer, Sherlee, & Ulanah, and my spiritual godparents Ocandenije and Oba Ekun.

To my sista-friend & colleague Kadija George Sesay and the other poets & creatives whose belief, insights, prompts and listening ears helped me birth these poems: Jean "Binta" Breeze, Malika Booker, Nadine Chambers, Jayne Cortez, Nkechi Ebite/The Books Project, Thomas Glave, Jardyn Lake, Sai Murray and Donna Aza Weir-Soley. Also the groups: Malika's Kitchen, Nka Iban, and my Barbados workshops with the Poui/Collymore poets and Code Red: For Gender Justice.

Thanks to Jeremy for his invaluable and ever-insightful editing; Hannah & Adam for design & marketing; my Peepal Tree family and our offspring the Inscribe Originals, Young Inscribers and the Inscribe Nationals.

DOROTHEA SMARTT

READER, I MARRIED HIM

& OTHER QUEER GOINGS-ON

PEEPAL TREE

First published in Great Britain in 2014
Peepal Tree Press Ltd
17 King's Avenue
Leeds LS6 1QS
UK

© Dorothea Smartt 2014

All rights reserved
No part of this publication may be
reproduced or transmitted in any form
without permission

ISBN 13: 9781845232870

CONTENTS

woman with golden apple (no ordinary fruit)	7
muriel	8
drawn to you	11
reader, i married him	12
full moon at the hot pot	14
precious…	15
sing girl! sing!	16
red shoes	18
telling time	19
headway	20
the trick they played was to be invisible…	21
eshu cuban fusion	22
is this a love poem?	23
on arrival at the royal college of music…	24
the yellow & black triangles	25
a sense of denial	26

woman with golden apple (no ordinary fruit)
after Lotte Kramer's *Boy With Orange (out of Kosovo)*

A woman holding a golden apple in her palms
has crossed the boundary, uncertain yet hopeful.

She waits there, glances back at stony ground – scenes
when her desire was too held in check, diminishing.

Now, with this globe she's grasping, something beckons;
its small oval assurance, a piquant promise of juiciness

no one shall deny. She dares a smile at signs of surrender
within her. Packed precariously about a soft-spiky seed.

Soon she will uncover the arousing body, touch tangy lips,
kiss a loving woman; traverse any stings of this asylum.

muriel

Damp sheets on wet brown bodies. Brown!? She was cinnamon-sweet-chocolate, smooth and creamy on my tongue's heat. I dived into you, sinking between cocoa arms, legs, thighs and breasts. I knew your music, willing me to dance. Drew me away from company I'd made, to the edge: your arena where white people rock to rhythms of their own,

outside the music. You and I live on the inside, echoing each other's moves. I see myself dancing: the Sista moved liked we did back home. Realize I'm smiling, drawn out to join her. I'm finally face to face, bathed in lights going in time with the music, a Masaii's deep black eyes, such bottomless rivers! Seducing the sun out, heat on our surface trickling

down to our depths, and we beamed. Her eyes were fresh. Self-conscious in my two-day old clothes, body and soul hungry to know this sista, to fill minutes, hours, days with her, right there and then dreams singing. She deserted me, gesturing to the DJ's corner, empty until she stood there. Mixing the next track, concentrating but looking up to check

me out where she'd left me. Did she want me to wait? I wanted to wait. I was waiting and watching some guy appear, talking to her. Those bottomless rivers surge through me again, sweeping over his shoulders. Music in place, she rolls back over, *Su-ma nay u?* Then *Amerikaans?* she offers. *No, London.* I said. A surprised *English!* came, stroking my face

Ahh Kribisi. She said: *You dance good. U beweegt zich als de liefde van! Hoe kom?! You are a sister!* I grin embarrassed by the caress of her voice. Replying: *I know! I saw you dancing and thought you were from London; you got the same moves I got!* So we danced on, sampling each other, drawing each other out. But then I remembered the blonde

German woman I arrived with. I spied her calling to me. Reluctant, wishing I'd come unattached, showed my Sista I had to go. Assured I wouldn't leave without coming back to her. Upstairs. Knocking back champagne overlooking assorted Amsterdam people. Someone passed me a joint, I dragged on, meditating on breaking loose. I was meant to be hustling for a place to stay. The white German woman, she'd done this loads of times, travel-wise to drinking and eating generously of everything offered. Imagine staying with the DJ! That thought shifted me from daydreams. I descended to dance more. We had to wait, til the place closed. It was a long walk to her studio, dropping into all-night

shops, talking to all-night people. Me: an irritated third in an unwelcome threesome. And then we were four – joined by a brother. They talked lively in their Surinamese, not Dutch. At her studio, while she slipped on Marvin Gaye, smoothing *Midnite Love*, on through the night. The other woman and I longed for bed but found not even a settee to rest on.

She seemed (not for the first time) to be listening to the brother's troubles, sky transforming through cups of coffee. Truly exhausted now, I looked again for a bed in her sparse space! The woman had to sleep! In one corner, shrouded in papyrus leaves taller than me, her whiter-than-white bathtub, deep glazed like asses milk. A tempting bed. We passed

out on her few cushions. It was full-on morning when she roused us. *Kom sribi* – he had finally left. *Nous allons au lit?* I hoped. Into the kitchenette! Where was she taking us now? I just needed to lie down. Waving us back, she knelt, pulling at a ring I'd not seen in the floor. Down. Under, inside to her bed below. To our hesitant two-way stares

she declared: *Dit is waar wij slapen. Aahh? – sommeil!* Once inside, the hatch drawn shut, we could only just sit up. I sandwiched between imaginings, slept restless. Muriel and I stirred together, lay speaking softly. Searching tongues – English-French-Dutch-Sranantongo – for understanding. Me: hot and happy for this moment. She: curious about

the woman I was with: *Your Uma? She is your "amie"?* she ventured. My *NON*! blurted out, loudly. *Safri taki!* she peered over me. Smiling, I said more softly, *We met travelling. Umm... Juste voyageant ensemble!* I don't remember how we started? Trusting she would understand a touch on a breast, a thigh pressing. Eyes tender with longing we could not sound, 'til I felt her quietly and my own melody touched hers. All the time staring cinnamon-sweet, her gentle bottomless rivers, quietly whispering *Welcome, Sisa*. Spreading her lips and thighs. Chocolate-cinnamon hands clearing the way, uncovered all my untouched places, doubt and indecision rolling back. The woman on my other side woke

to murmuring movements, my prayer that said: *This is no place for you*. To my relief she left. We did not stop to ask her where, only glancing briefly as we heard the door slam. I have you to myself, caramel-smooth, creamy. I dive further, willing, knowing. Submerged between sepia-umber breasts, our music making me twirl. Trying each other out in our

laughter, echoing moves, body and soul coming to know this Sista, passing minutes, hours, days with her right there and then. Damp sheets on wet brown bodies.

drawn to you

Oya: You got to be you.
Shango: That's what I say. Always be you…
People fit together different
I fit with you different than I fit with other people,
I got something drawing to you, and I feel you drawing to me
Shango curls his finger around Oya's ear and
caresses the soft…
    In The Red & Brown Water — Tarell Alvin McCraney

Easy now. No need to push-pull   let it be.
I got something drawing to you
and I feel you drawing to me.
We fit together, different   yet we
make a pair, lassoed with each others fears,
loving. Easy now. Not so easy now,
tripping over myself, something drawing me.
I fit with you different
than I fit with women
I love – it's all me though –
the parts I hold in, the parts I lay out,
the places we meet, don't
tolerate, that meld and repel.
Still. Feel you drawing to me and
I got something drawing to you,
curling its fingers around, caressing
the soft   easy.

reader, i married him

Reader, I married him.
A son with his father's name,
loving a man twice his age,
hiding from dem men that kill
he las' "fren" – and chop-he
widda a machete! Slice scarring he face
impairing he eyes (like a Mr. Rochester)
but not mine. I could see a way, clear-clear.

Reader, I married him
so he could lef outta JA. Take refuge
in my British citizenship,
my redundant heterosex right
to marry any man. So I flew to Bim,
to do it beachside, tropical style –
at least in the photos
that would serve as proof.

Reader, I married him.
My best man? His lover, gave me away,
was wedding planner, witness,
and his wedding night delight,
man enough to cover every detail
of our act. Rehearsing Junior
in his role. For this was a political act:
I was the lifeboat, love boat.

Reader I married him,
this young guy half my age.
The Bajan registrar looked weary
at another "rent-a-dread" giving
"Stella-her-groove-back".
I was a politically incorrect act:

bewitch, turn-head tourist trapped
by his honey eyes, glazed by my island man.

Reader, I married him.
I was confident, self-assured, but
still feigning new love coyness.
He was all fingers and thumbs,
dumb in the face of her authority.
Me, the blushing brown-skin bride,
who produced the rings, asked
his lover for the wedding bands.

Reader, I married him – for love
of our humanity. Arms entwined,
we sipped each other's champagne,
clutching me between Sandy Lane's columns –
our photographer sneaking kisses.
Reader, I married him, played a part
for a JA brother. Reader I, married him.
With our *tainted love* we said, "I do."

full moon at the hot pot

men cruise
taking each other
in with the sulphur
waters lapping
eager glowing bodies
one stretched
on moon-bathed sands
waits for the right man
to ease his ache

precious...

like I'm old gold. Her hands
heat places that cave in
softly, to fine molten. Swirling,

I gleam. A-blaze sweat
voices, sounds of her other lips
sexy on my tongue. Turning

with her sighs, she brings
me back. Making me all new.
Her body, polishing me –

solid now – bright and fine
again.

sing girl! sing!

Sing girl, sing! – First
breathe. Let it out, the sound
from the bell, from the base,
from the thorax, opening. Sing,
work that first instrument
of humanity, and sing!
Say sing in any language
and the truth will out!
Sing: play that first
instrument of the blues, of
pain, of the yellow high-
up, sun-leaping joyous sounds.
Can you hold a note?
Like a Tibetan, circular breathing,
chanting? Can you click like a Xhosa?
Intone like a Bulgarian belle?
Beautiful
is in the mouth
of the sayer.
Like a harmonica
like a jew's harp
like a whistle
like a bow on a string-sing,
work that first instrument
hone it, form the notes
on a scale of "doh" to "tee", 5:4,
8:8, 16 beats to a bar, flow
like a star shower,
like a roaring river, howl
like a tumultuous tornado,
soar eagle high. Sing alone
and in unison, a chorus-line.
Work-it sister-girl, work
that first instrument, bring

me joy, bring me sorrow,
mark the occasion, the passage,
any rite with sounds.
Where people gather
won't be too long before
someone starts a song.
It's natural! It's native, it's
normal to work the voice
beyond speech, wavering with
sound shapes of words.
From the deep beyond
the throat and windpipe,
hums, trills, screams,
booms, bellows
punctuate, accentuate,
resound, reverberate,
replay again and again,
sound over sound – polyvocal,
polyrhythmic – echo, soar,
sigh, gasp! Exhale. Inhale.
Sing – sensation oozing
through the mouth, beyond
lyrics, beyond thought, beyond!
Unleash that first instrument,
work the breath, your chest, your
diaphragm, your lungs and

sing girl!
Sing!

red shoes

Clack-clack! Girls' pulverized bound feet,
a whiff of jasmine. Face a mask of pain.
Tap-tap! The ballet blocks in *The Red Shoes*
scared me. Her Svengali-master thrusting
his cane into the dance-floor, as she moved
to his beat. Her toes bloody on their blocks.
Click-click! To Kansas. Dorothy's heels sparkle
technicolor incongruous, with her little-girl garb.

A Black girl's feet seem to hold no allure.
No fetish fodder. Not covetable.
Relieved, I slip them in red Birkenstocks!
Blatantly, park them on double yellow lines.

telling time

The girls in the motion pictures
are older women now in their best
dressed blue-rinses, watching
their senior men, bald crowns shining,
with their young side by side, nodding
as their families see their years slip away.

headway

> …down near the jetty where fishgutfunk fumed furiously…
> *The African Origins of UFOs* — Anthony Joseph

The time was ripe. Heal me. Lead me willingly down,
out past deceits, to our own brand of salvation. The near-
east, far-east, western, native American, the aboriginal, the
"Egyptian" ,wells of oneness missing a voice. Out on the jetty
of my life so far, I'd had to wonder. I glimpsed below where
swirling swarms of hoodoo-voodoo priests, fetish fishgutfunk
witch-doctors, obeah men, pocomania roots women fumed
at their muddied fount. Undeterred, making headway, furiously.

the trick they played was to be invisible…

With three rings
of cigar smoke,

my London and New York City
waft into *Ilé-Ifè.**

My shoes carried me full circle.
At this opening, I bare my soles,

connect with Earth.

---

* *Ifè*, also *Ilé-Ifè*: An ancient Yoruba city in south-western Nigeria, associated with the centre of Lucumi/Santeria in the New World. The meaning of the word "ifè" in the Yoruba language is "expansion"; "Ilé-Ifè" is therefore a reference to the myth of origin, "The Land of Expansion". http://en.wikipedia.org/wiki/Ife

eshu* cuban fusion

The squat Eshu cook works the kitchen,
mischievous with gender,
Is you is or is you ain't? Hermanos? Hermana?
Flicking ash with a flourished question mark,
turning back to steamy pots –
what they do best – mixing, stirring
ingredients to make something
altogether enhancing to the taste.

---

*Eshu – an energy/deity that reflects a manifestations of The Divine, from the Yoruba spiritual-religious system and related New World traditions. The spirit of chaos and trickery, raising mortals' awareness through experiences that lead ultimately to their maturation. Trickster figures can often exhibit gender and form variability, changing gender roles, and even occasionally engaging in same-sex practices.
http://en.wikipedia.org/wiki/Eshu
http://en.wikipedia.org/wiki/Orisha
http://en.wikipedia.org/wiki/Trickery

is this a love poem?

The Alexandria taxi driver gifted us
with music as he swayed
through the traffic with hyphenated Africans,
shorthaired diaspora women riding
in his black and white
fixed again and again FIAT.

A city stretched along the Mediterranean,
home to a woman's voice,
not like the pop artists on my telly,
her sound is a legacy of Andalusia,
grander, larger than time.
Flying back down The Corniche

we stop again, her voice still playing,
towards the walls of the Palace Hotel
and my only Egyptian full moon.
I sleep with curtains pulled back,
wishing the moon to cross me as I dream,
to see sunrise after the moonlight

with her music still swaying me
from my page, syllables of Egyptian-Arabic
sweet sounds snaking my hips around;
my rationality to somewhere beyond
to where love lets me believe, faith lets me fly.

on arrival at the royal college of music...

For Samuel Coleridge Taylor, Afro-British composer, 1875-1912.

Samuel entered the auditorium, notes soaring in his head.
"Mister Taylor!" the sarcastic voice from the front boomed,

"So glad you decided to join us!" The music room's clock
seemed to tick like a metronome, breaking the spell.

"My sincerest apologies, Professor. Please be assured
my tardiness is no reflection on my deepest respect

for yourself, and my fellow gentlemen student musicians –
and you, of course, Madame." He inclined his head to her,

ever so gently, casting his deep black eyes down her face.
Jessica looked up! Her eyes fell first on his black boots

polished to the hilt, his white shirt all the whiter
against his sable skin. She realised she was holding her

breath. As the bronzed face descended to meet her gaze,
the music room's clock seem to "tock" like a metronome,

the click of his heels, in rhythm, making the "tick".
He, so in sync! His hair a dark splendid mass! A halo

she wanted to touch. Samuel sat as close by as seating
permitted. Jessica, blushing, bowed her head in her notes.

the yellow & black triangles
after Frank O'Hara's *Les Etiquettes Jaune*

A leaf came down on my lap
today in Hyde Park.
Is this of no consequence?

Leaf! You are one of many!
Did you choose your
colour, then choose me

as if there was such
a thing as kismet?

You are too unconcerned
to answer. I am lonely
enough to insist.

Leaf! Don't you ignore
our colour; pretend it's
me that's high-strung.

a sense of denial

Denial looks black, panelled, silver-edged
and gleaming. Car-washed in water,
enough to quench a dying village's thirst,
a Hummer, petrol guzzling in a London traffic jam,
its darkened windows seal out the day's cool breeze,
to keep in an air-con fool, a lone driver in his third car –
the one that's just for fun! The tread of the rubber
tyres bouncing me back to trees tapped
of their strength to let us breathe.

Denial is the clicking of a million light switches
going on as the sun sets in the North (and scorches the South),
a single home lit by countless careless bulbs,
the hum of its appliances on stand-by. While
clicking fingers coat the keys of a Playstation,
and a car chase roars from the DVD on the plasma screen,
someone else plugs into a symphony of jungalist beats.

Denial is the burning smell of toast,
a third round of single slices under a gas grill,
or the blackened, burnt-out wreck of once Ogoni land;
or, stepping out into the city's morning traffic fumes,
smog clogging a child's breath, inhaler at the ready,
stopping to pick up the rich roast of coffee in a Starbucks' mug,
and an oversized, under-nourishing Big Mac for lunch.

Denial is tasteless, with a dash of MSG making all falsified
flavours more amplified – even the blandness of the water-fat
injected chicken, with enough legs for everyone,
coated in orange crumbs that were never bread,
garnished with a mutated modified tomato, ever-fresh
and tasteless on the tongue, plumped in polystyrene buns.

Denial could feel warming, a cosy carcinogenic electric
blanket heating up the cold night under thin sheets,
or slippery like okra or egg yolk, never to be held,
grasped in the fingers. Denial could feel rough
like concrete, like a West Bank wall,
watchtower beams glaring in the dark, like
waters diverted from the Gaza Strip to irrigate
agriculture for an all but gated community,
Dobermans in the yard, security cameras rolling.

Denial is in that air-conditioned Miami house,
sitting in a sweater on a 90 degree day, then
piling a half-load of wet clothes into a dryer –
or in Reading, taking the car across the road
to buy a newspaper. Denial is walking London's streets
complaining about the price of petrol and rising taxes,
anxious to jet-set to another, anonymous, exotic sunny beach.

ABOUT THE AUTHOR

Dorothea Smartt is a literary activist, live artist, established and respected poet with an international reputation. Born and raised in London she is described as a "Brit-born Bajan international". With two full collections, *Connecting Medium* and *Ship Shape* (Peepal Tree Press) her years of experience, include engagements with the British Council in Bahrain, South Africa, USA, Egypt, and Hungary. In 2013 she was keynote speaker at the Barbados Frank Collymore Literary Endowment Award. She is an honorary team member and advisor to Cambridge University's Caribbean Poetry Project. She is Co-Director of Inscribe: national writer development programme, Associate Poetry Editor of "Sable Litmag", guest co-editor of their LGBTQI issues, and an Advisory editor to "Scarf", a global arts & literature magazine. In her forthcoming third collection she continues to rework standard narratives, this time examining same-sex relationships and cross-gender experiences as push-pull factors behind "West Indian" émigré workers on the Panama Canal.